Antonio VIVALDI

(1678 – 1741)

Sonata No. 5 for Cello and Basso continuo (Piano), RV 40
E minor / mi mineur / e-moll

Edited by
Josef Hofer

DOWANI International

Preface

This volume presents Antonio Vivaldi's Sonata No. 5 for cello and basso continuo in E minor (RV 40), a splendid example of the Venetian master's inexhaustible powers of invention. The mood of the second *Largo* is especially impressive; its straightforward harmonies and its limitation to a few motifs place the movement in the near vicinity of the "Four Seasons". Vivaldi's cello sonatas are among his most venturesome works, and it is no surprise that they belong to the standard repertoire of every cellist. Their melodic range encompasses the first four positions and can be managed by moderately advanced learners. Our edition enables you to learn the work systematically at various tempos with piano accompaniment.

The CD opens with the concert version of each movement (cello and piano). After tuning your instrument (Track 1), the musical work can begin. First, you will hear the piano accompaniment at slow and medium tempo for practice purposes. At slow tempo you can also hear the cello played softly in the background as a guide. Having mastered these levels, you can now play the piece with piano accompaniment at the original tempo. Each movement has been sensibly divided into subsections for practice purposes. You can select the subsection you want using the track numbers indicated in the solo part. Further explanations can be found at the end of this volume along with the names of the musicians involved in the recording. More detailed information can be found in the Internet at www.dowani.com. All of the versions were recorded live.

The fingering and bowing marks in this edition were provided by Josef Hofer, a cellist and teacher living in Liechtenstein. Hofer studied with Walter Grimmer in Berne and Gerhard Mantel in Frankfurt am Main. He is well known as a chamber musician and jury member at various national and international competitions and has taught for many years in Liechtenstein and Switzerland.

We wish you lots of fun playing from our *DOWANI 3 Tempi Play Along* editions and hope that your musicality and diligence will enable you to play the concert version as soon as possible. Our goal is to provide the essential conditions you need for effective practicing through motivation, enjoyment and fun.

Your DOWANI Team

Avant-propos

Avec cette édition nous vous présentons la sonate n° 5 pour violoncelle et basse continue RV 40 en mi mineur d'Antonio Vivaldi qui démontre la créativité inépuisable du maître vénitien. L'ambiance du deuxième *Largo* est particulièrement impressionnante. Les harmonisations épurées et la limitation à peu de motifs rappellent les "Quatre Saisons". Les sonates pour violoncelle font partie des œuvres les plus expérimentales de Vivaldi. C'est pourquoi les sonates font partie du répertoire de base de chaque violoncelliste. La présente sonate utilise les premières quatre positions et peut être jouée par des élèves un peu avancés. Notre édition vous offre la possibilité de travailler l'œuvre d'une manière systématique dans différents tempos avec accompagnement de piano.

Le CD vous permettra d'entendre d'abord la version de concert de chaque mouvement (violoncelle et piano). Après avoir accordé votre instrument (plage n° 1), vous pourrez commencer le travail musical. Pour travailler le morceau au tempo lent et au tempo moyen, vous entendrez l'accompagnement de piano. Au tempo lent, le violoncelle restera cependant toujours audible très doucement à l'arrière-plan. Vous pourrez ensuite jouer le tempo original avec accompagnement de piano. Chaque mouvement a été divisé en sections judicieuses pour faciliter le travail. Vous pouvez sélectionner ces sections à l'aide des numéros de plages indiqués dans la partie du soliste. Pour obtenir plus d'informations et les noms des artistes qui ont participé aux enregistrements, veuillez consulter la dernière page de cette édition ou notre site Internet : www.dowani.com. Toutes les versions ont été enregistrées en direct.

Les doigtés et indications des coups d'archet proviennent du violoncelliste et pédagogue Josef Hofer qui vit au Liechtenstein. Il étudia auprès de Walter Grimmer à Berne et Gerhard Mantel à Francfort-sur-le-Main. Josef Hofer est musicien de chambre et membre de jury de divers concours nationaux et internationaux. Il enseigne depuis de nombreuses années au Liechtenstein et en Suisse.

Nous vous souhaitons beaucoup de plaisir à faire de la musique avec la collection *DOWANI 3 Tempi Play Along* et nous espérons que votre musicalité et votre application vous amèneront aussi rapidement que possible à la version de concert. Notre but est de vous offrir les bases nécessaires pour un travail efficace par la motivation et le plaisir.

Les Éditions DOWANI

Vorwort

Mit dieser Ausgabe präsentieren wir Ihnen die Sonate Nr. 5 für Violoncello und Basso continuo RV 40 in e-moll von Antonio Vivaldi, die den unerschöpflichen Ideenreichtum des venezianischen Meisters zeigt. Besonders eindrücklich ist die Stimmung des zweiten *Largo*. Die Schlichtheit der Harmonik und die Beschränkung auf wenige Motive rücken diesen Satz in die Nähe der „Vier Jahreszeiten". Die Vivaldi-Sonaten für Cello gehören zu den experimentierfreudigsten Werken Vivaldis. Nicht umsonst gehören diese Sonaten zum Standardrepertoire eines jeden Cellisten. Der Tonraum umfasst die ersten vier Lagen und kann von leicht fortgeschrittenen Schülern bewältigt werden. Diese Ausgabe ermöglicht es Ihnen, das Werk systematisch und in verschiedenen Tempi mit Klavierbegleitung zu erarbeiten.

Auf der CD hören Sie zuerst die Konzertversion eines jeden Satzes (Violoncello und Klavier). Nach dem Stimmen Ihres Instrumentes (Track 1) kann die musikalische Arbeit beginnen. Zum Üben folgt nun im langsamen und mittleren Tempo die Klavierbegleitung, wobei im langsamen Tempo das Cello als Orientierung leise im Hintergrund zu hören ist. Anschließend können Sie sich im Originaltempo vom Klavier begleiten lassen. Jeder Satz wurde in sinnvolle Übe-Abschnitte unterteilt. Diese können Sie mit Hilfe der in der Solostimme angegebenen Track-Nummern auswählen. Weitere Erklärungen hierzu sowie die Namen der Künstler finden Sie auf der letzten Seite dieser Ausgabe; ausführlichere Informationen können Sie im Internet unter www.dowani.com nachlesen. Alle eingespielten Versionen wurden live aufgenommen.

Die Fingersätze und Striche in dieser Ausgabe stammen von dem in Liechtenstein lebenden Cellisten und Pädagogen Josef Hofer. Er studierte bei Walter Grimmer in Bern sowie bei Gerhard Mantel in Frankfurt am Main. Josef Hofer ist als Kammermusiker und Jurymitglied bei diversen nationalen und internationalen Wettbewerben tätig und unterrichtet seit vielen Jahren in Liechtenstein und der Schweiz.

Wir wünschen Ihnen viel Spaß beim Musizieren mit unseren *DOWANI 3 Tempi Play Along*-Ausgaben und hoffen, dass Ihre Musikalität und Ihr Fleiß Sie möglichst bald bis zur Konzertversion führen werden. Unser Ziel ist es, Ihnen durch Motivation, Freude und Spaß die notwendigen Voraussetzungen für effektives Üben zu schaffen.

Ihr DOWANI Team

Antonio
VIVALDI

(1678 – 1741)

Sonata No. 5 for Cello and Basso continuo (Piano), RV 40
E minor / mi mineur / e-moll

Cello / Violoncelle / Violoncello

DOWANI International

Cello

Sonata No. 5

for Cello and Basso continuo (Piano), RV 40

E minor / mi mineur / e-moll

A. Vivaldi (1678 – 1741)

Edited by J. Hofer

DOW 3501

4

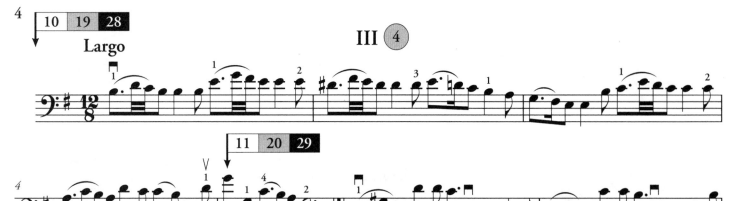

2

Antonio VIVALDI

(1678 – 1741)

Sonata No. 5 for Cello and Basso continuo (Piano), RV 40
E minor / mi mineur / e-moll

Basso continuo / Basse continue / Generalbass

DOWANI International

Sonata No. 5

for Cello and Basso continuo (Piano), RV 40

E minor / mi mineur / e-moll

A. Vivaldi (1678 – 1741)

I

II

III

4

IV

Sonata No. 5

for Cello and Basso continuo (Piano), RV 40
E minor / mi mineur / e-moll

A. Vivaldi (1678 – 1741)
Continuo Realization: G. Stöver

DOW 3501

8

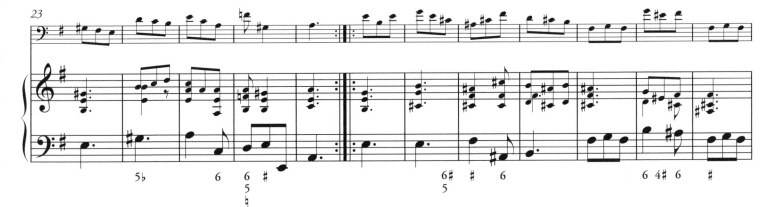

ENGLISH

DOWANI CD:
- Track No. 1
- Track numbers in circles
- Track numbers in squares

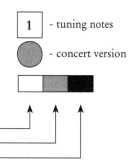

$\boxed{1}$ - tuning notes

⬤ - concert version

- slow Play Along Tempo
- intermediate Play Along Tempo
- original Play Along Tempo

- Additional tracks for longer movements or pieces
- **Concert version:** cello and piano
- **Slow tempo:** piano accompaniment with cello in the background
- **Intermediate tempo:** piano accompaniment only
- **Original tempo:** piano accompaniment only

Please note that the recorded version of the piano accompaniment may differ slightly from the sheet music. This is due to the spontaneous character of live music making and the artistic freedom of the musicians. The original sheet music for the solo part is, of course, not affected.

FRANÇAIS

DOWANI CD:
- Plage N° 1
- N° de plage dans un cercle
- N° de plage dans un rectangle

$\boxed{1}$ - diapason

⬤ - version de concert

- tempo lent play along
- tempo moyen play along
- tempo original play along

- Plages supplémentaires pour mouvements ou morceaux longs
- **Version de concert :** violoncelle et piano
- **Tempo lent :** accompagnement de piano avec violoncelle en fond sonore
- **Tempo moyen :** seulement l'accompagnement de piano
- **Tempo original :** seulement l'accompagnement de piano

L'enregistrement de l'accompagnement de piano peut présenter quelques différences mineures par rapport au texte de la partition. Ceci est du à la liberté artistique des musiciens et résulte d'un jeu spontané et vivant, mais n'affecte, bien entendu, d'aucune manière la partie soliste.

DEUTSCH

DOWANI CD:
- Track Nr. 1
- Trackangabe im Kreis
- Trackangabe im Rechteck

$\boxed{1}$ - Stimmtöne

⬤ - Konzertversion

- langsames Play Along Tempo
- mittleres Play Along Tempo
- originales Play Along Tempo

- Zusätzliche Tracks bei längeren Sätzen oder Stücken
- **Konzertversion:** Violoncello und Klavier
- **Langsames Tempo:** Klavierbegleitung mit Violoncello im Hintergrund
- **Mittleres Tempo:** nur Klavierbegleitung
- **Originaltempo:** nur Klavierbegleitung

Die Klavierbegleitung auf der CD-Aufnahme kann gegenüber dem Notentext kleine Abweichungen aufweisen. Dies geht in der Regel auf die künstlerische Freiheit der Musiker und auf spontanes, lebendiges Musizieren zurück. Die Solostimme bleibt davon selbstverständlich unangetastet.

DOWANI - 3 Tempi Play Along is published by:
DOWANI International Est.
Industriestrasse 24 / Postfach 156, FL-9487 Bendern,
Principality of Liechtenstein
Phone: ++423 370 11 15, Fax ++423 370 19 44
Email: info@dowani.com
www.dowani.com

Recording & Digital Mastering: Pavel Lavrenenkov, Russia
CD-Production: MediaMotion, The Netherlands
Music Notation: Notensatz Thomas Metzinger, Germany
Design: Andreas Haselwanter, Austria
Printed by: Zrinski d.d., Croatia
Made in the Principality of Liechtenstein

Concert Version
Sergey Sudzilovsky, Cello
Vitaly Junitsky, Piano

3 Tempi Accompaniment
Slow:
Vitaly Junitsky, Piano

Intermediate:
Vitaly Junitsky, Piano

Original:
Vitaly Junitsky, Piano